P I L G R I

✠

RIEVAULX
FOUNTAINS
BYLAND & JERVAULX

Other titles available in this series

PILGRIM · GUIDE

RIEVAULX
FOUNTAINS
BYLAND & JERVAULX

The Cistercian Abbeys of North Yorkshire

Lucy Beckett

Illustrated by
Martyn Beckett

CANTERBURY
PRESS
Norwich

Text © Lucy Beckett 1998
Illustrations © Martyn Beckett 1998

First published in 1998 by The Canterbury Press Norwich
(a publishing imprint of Hymns Ancient & Modern Limited
a registered charity)
St Mary's Works, St Mary's Plain
Norwich, Norfolk NR3 3BH

British Library Cataloguing in Publication Data

A catalogue record for this book is available
from the British Library

ISBN 1-85311-202-X

Typeset by Rowland Phototypesetting Ltd,
Bury St Edmunds, Suffolk IP32 6NU
Printed and bound in Great Britain by
Redwood Books, Trowbridge, Wilts

Contents

Preface

A visitor to any of the ruined Cistercian abbeys of
North Yorkshire will not find it difficult to grasp the
layout of the main buildings: the church, the cloister,
the chapter-house; the refectory, the dormitory, the
lay-brothers' range. This layout is roughly the same
in every Cistercian abbey, not only in Yorkshire but
throughout Europe. Those who look after the
Yorkshire abbeys have provided excellent plans,
notices and guidebooks to help the visitor under-
stand the ruins. But for many people, struck and perhaps moved by the peaceful, timeless atmosphere of
these great wrecked buildings, left behind in the
countryside by an ancient way of living, questions
will remain.

How did these abbeys, home for centuries to hun-
dreds of monks, come to be here? Who built them,
financed them? How did the people who lived in
them spend their days? What inspired them to leave
the everyday world for a difficult, disciplined life
lived in a single place in obedience to a Rule and an
abbot? Who were the great men of this story? Can
we, who live in a noisier, faster-moving world than

they did, learn something from them? What is it?

This *Pilgrim Guide* attempts to answer these questions. The abbeys were built, stone by stone, by people and for people, to pray in, to work in, to live in. The stones that remain are beautiful, but their beauty has to do with the people who here, in these wild places, put their whole lives in the hands of God. It is the holiness of this intention, and of many lives lived in these abbeys, that can still make a pilgrim out of any visitor to their ruins.

Standard plan of a twelfth-century Cistercian abbey

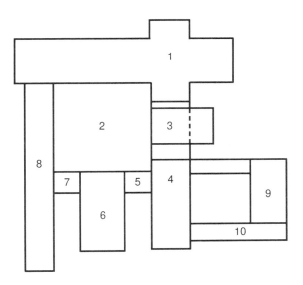

Key

1 Church
2 Cloister
3 Chapter-house
4 Monks' dormitory (dorter) above
5 Warming room (calefactory)
6 Monks' refectory (frater)
7 Kitchen
8 Lay-brothers' range
9 Infirmary
10 Latrines (reredorter)

1

Historical Background

Rievaulx: the abbey church in winter

In 1066, when William the Conqueror took control of England after the Battle of Hastings, there was not a single monastery north of a line from Worcester to the Wash.

Four centuries earlier the old Kingdom of

Northumbria, which then stretched all the way from the Humber to the Firth of Forth, had seen an extraordinary flowering of Christian monastic life. In 563, not long after the death of St Benedict at Monte Cassino in Italy, soon to be destroyed by raiding Lombards, St Columba arrived in Iona from Ireland with a dozen monks. These were Celtic monks, leading a simple missionary life, teaching Christianity to still pagan people and training boys to become monks and priests. They had never heard of St Benedict.

From this modest beginning there developed, in the next 200 years, the golden age of monks in the north-east of England: St Aidan and St Cuthbert at Lindisfarne; St Chad and St Cedd, monk-bishops and founders of monasteries; St Hilda presiding over her nuns and monks at Whitby, where the Celtic and Roman traditions were united in the Synod of 664; St Wilfrid at Ripon and Hexham, whose monks were the first in the north to live according to the Roman Rule of St Benedict; St Benet Biscop, whose journeys to Rome furnished his monasteries at Jarrow and Wearmouth with the books and scholarship that made possible the writing of his pupil St Bede; Alcuin of York, who educated Charlemagne's court and died as Abbot of Tours on the Loire. This was a golden age of monastic living, monastic learning and monastic enterprise unequalled at the time anywhere else in what had been the western Roman empire.

But in 1066 some ruins, and some books,

particularly Bede's *Ecclesiastical History of the English People*, were all that was left of this great period in the history of the Church in England. At York and Durham there were battered cathedral churches, their liturgy sustained by groups of priests, some married, but no 'regular' (i.e. according to a Rule) religious life. Viking invaders, for whom monks and their undefended churches were easy prey, had wiped the monasteries of the north-east from the map. Anglo-Saxon Christianity just held on in the region, though Viking York became the most pagan city in the whole of the Danelaw. But when in the tenth century St Dunstan, Archbishop of Canterbury, and his fellow monk-bishops revived monastic life in the southern half of England, the dangerous and thinly populated north remained untouched by their efforts. The last time Viking raiders sailed up the Ouse and burnt the Minster in York was in 1075, nine years after the Norman Conquest.

William the Conqueror's Normans were Vikings themselves. But in north-western France, as converts to Christianity, they had already organized a flourishing diocesan and monastic life. This experience, along with their enthusiasm for the new, for construction, for strong feudal connections binding society together, meant that the Normans came to England to build, not to destroy. This was not an invasion in the sense of a large-scale movement of population. A small number of powerful Normans came to rule the English people, not to displace them.

3

They ruled them pretty efficiently, and stayed for good, Norman bishops and abbots taking control of the sees and major monasteries of the country, and a great monk, Lanfranc of Bec, Archbishop of Canterbury, running the English Church for William in a wise and humane fashion.

William himself did some terrifying destroying of his own in the north-east before he was satisfied that he would be obeyed there. In January 1069 a party of Norman soldiers was massacred in Durham and the whole of Northumbria looked likely to rebel against the new government. William himself stormed up with a strong force from the south and his revenge on the north-east was savage and thorough. The old Bishop of Durham fled with his clergy and the precious bones of St Cuthbert to Lindisfarne, and the cathedral was left empty except for the wounded and dying.

On the ancient road that follows the escarpment of the Hambleton Hills above Rievaulx and Byland Abbeys, William and his bullying soldiers got separated one night in a blizzard. The furious king was found in the morning rampaging alone among the snowdrifts. 'As cold as Billy Norman' is a local phrase to this day.

The 'harrying of the north' in 1069 did nothing, at first, to encourage the sense of security and protection from violence that monks need if they are to live a peaceful, holy life. But soon the Norman grip on the whole of England was firm enough for a new beginning to be made, even in the scarred and desolate north-east.

The first monks to take advantage of the new Norman order in the north were three Anglo-Saxon Benedictines from the quiet heart of old monastic Wessex. Brought up on Bede, wanting to restore something of the glorious monastic past of Northumbria, they set out from Winchcombe and Evesham in 1073 and, after a shaky start, managed to refound Jarrow, and a little later Wearmouth and Whitby. From Whitby in 1078 the Benedictine Abbey of St Mary's in York was founded, close to the new Norman Minster. It soon became a rich and powerful house. Meanwhile at Durham, where the relics of St Cuthbert had at last been laid to rest, a strong Norman monk-bishop had founded the great Benedictine cathedral priory with monks from Jarrow and Wearmouth.

This was the new monastic picture in the north-east of England when the third Norman king, Henry I, gave the estate of Helmsley to a loyal baron, Walter Espec, on the understanding that he would help to defend England and the Norman settlement against any remaining disaffection. There were Benedictines in the cathedral cities to the north and to the south of Ryedale and the Yorkshire moors. But the moors and dales themselves were wild, forested land. Few people lived in this difficult country, particularly since William I's fierce onslaught – the Domesday survey of 1086 suggests that about seventy people were then living in the whole of upper Ryedale. A little village church like that of Helmsley must have had a hard time sustaining the simplest Christian routine for the people.

Meanwhile a new ferment was working in the lives of all bishops, priests and monks. In the second half of the eleventh century, just as William I was getting a firm hold on his newly conquered England, the whole Latin Church was undergoing a vigorous reform. A succession of tough, independent-minded popes set themselves to raise the moral tone of every diocese and every parish, to free the Church from the interference of kings and emperors, and to make sure that traditional entanglements with the lay world of wealthy families, privilege and inheritance were unravelled so that the Church could run its own affairs.

One consequence of this reform movement was a fresh wind blowing through monastic life. Several small groups of monks in Italy and then in France left their comfortable, well-endowed Benedictine abbeys and took to a rougher, more austere life in the mountains, woods and flooding levels of the coun-tryside, returning to the simplicity of life that they felt St Benedict had in mind when he wrote his Rule nearly 600 years before.

From one such group, living in the Burgundian hills, developed, after a hesitant start, the most successful new religious order of the time – the Cistercians. They were called after their first abbey,

Cîteaux, which was built on an inhospitable marsh. (The Latin for 'marsh' is *cisterna* – hence the French name Cîteaux.) By 1119, twenty-one years after the original group left their abbey of Molesme, there were ten Cistercian monasteries in France, and the whole Church was impressed by the quality of the life lived by their monks and by the inspiring zeal of their most striking abbot, Bernard of Clairvaux. When Bernard died in 1153 there were 339 Cistercian monasteries in western Christendom – a burgeoning growth of dusted-down religious life unparalleled in the history of the Church.

Bernard, a Burgundian nobleman, had started his monastic life as a novice in 1112. Just three years later he was appointed the founding abbot of a new monastery, and was to become the most powerful preacher and the most influential churchman of the twelfth century. But the vital organizing document of the Cistercian order, which held all its monasteries together in a structure of supervision and support which the Benedictine abbeys had never had, was written not by Bernard but by an English monk, Stephen Harding, one of the original Molesme defectors. Between them, Harding's *Carta Caritatis* ('Charter of Love') and the inspiration of Bernard's personality and holiness gave the Church the new monastic impetus which was in tune with the whole reform movement, and which that movement had made possible.

Far away from Burgundy in the wilds of

Yorkshire, Walter Espec heard of these splendid new monks and offered a small band of them, from Bernard's own community at Clairvaux, the wooded valley of the Rye above Helmsley so that they could found a new abbey in just the sort of challenging, uncultivated country they preferred. A stirring letter from Bernard to Henry I probably initiated the venture, and the project was warmly supported by Thurstan, one of the most distinguished of all archbishops of York. One Cistercian foundation had already been made in the south of England, at Waverley in Surrey, but it was in the north, now almost empty of the monastic presence that had once been so important to it, that the Cistercians made the great spiritual and social impact that still seems to echo in the ruins of their abbeys.

2

Rievaulx Abbey

Rievaulx: the choir of the church across the abbey fishpond

On 5 March 1132 twelve monks from Clairvaux, some of them French, some of them originally from Yorkshire, arrived in the valley at Rievaulx to begin Cistercian life in the north of England. They had visited Thurstan in York on their way, and were led by their newly appointed abbot, himself a Yorkshire-man. His name was William (outside the nobility almost no one had a surname in the twelfth century:

Stephen Harding was probably called something like Earding as an Englishman and Stephen when he got to France). William had been Master of the Minster school in York, and had gone to Bernard's Clairvaux, with Thurstan's blessing, to become a Cistercian monk. He had worked as Bernard's secretary, and no doubt liked the idea of taking a new foundation to his native country. What this little group of monks had to contend with when they first arrived can easily be imagined.

Early March in North Yorkshire is usually cold, windy and wet. Snow may have been lying on the ground. Many freezing nights lay ahead before the reliable beginning of warm spring weather. Probably some wooden huts had been prepared in a clearing on the valley floor for the monks arriving from so far, but the simplest shelter is all they would have had as they contemplated their new home and the heavy work ahead.

It was already the custom for Cistercians, as it had been for Benedictines in Normandy and England for the last fifty years or so, to begin their new monastery by building, first, a temporary wooden chapel, because every day Mass must be celebrated and the Office said, and then a stone church. Early Cistercian churches (one, Fontenay Abbey in Burgundy, built in the same decade as the Rievaulx church, survives intact for us to see just what they were like) were built in a special Cistercian form of the splendid, strong Romanesque style, always called 'Norman' in England, that was the current architectural manner in the whole of western Christendom.

But, in accordance with Cistercian principles of simplicity and austerity, their first churches, built in the 1120s and 1130s, were without any adornment of their powerful, peaceful structure. Tall, very slightly pointed arches, supported by heavy piers, formed a long, wide nave with side-aisles. The nave was only dimly lit by small windows. Transepts on similar lines with a squat tower over the crossing, and a plain square-ended chancel, completed the church. At Rievaulx we can now see, of that first dark, simple church, only the bases of the columns that once supported the nave arches, the remains, to a low level, of the outside walls of the nave, and the west walls of the transepts up to the level where later building, in whiter stone and with pointed windows, takes over. But enough of the first church is left to give us a clear idea of the scale and long duration of the work involved. A lot of this work would have been done by the monks themselves with, no doubt, some skilled masons to direct operations and a growing band of lay-brothers to help with the manual labour.

The little community at Rievaulx began very quickly to increase in numbers. It took no more than thirty-years for there to be 140 choir monks at Rievaulx. These were educated men, able to sing the full monastic Office – the psalms and canticles, Scripture readings and prayers laid down by

11

St Benedict in his Rule to take place at eight set hours of every day and night of a monk's life. At the end of the same thirty years there were also about 500 lay-brothers in the community which William and his dozen companions had begun. Some Benedictine and other monastic communities had had a few lay-brothers in the past. But one of the keys to the astonishing growth of the Cistercian order in the twelfth century was the much greater emphasis placed by its abbots on the lay-brothers' vocation.

Cistercian lay-brothers were unlearned men (not necessarily peasants; many Norman knights could not read) with little or no Latin. Their experience of a call to the monastic life was nevertheless fully recognized by the Cistercians. This recognition was combined with the desire of the whole order to avoid unnecessary involvement with the ordinary land-owning world of tenants, serfs and house-servants. So the encouragement of lay-brothers to live as part of the monastic community, with a much simpler liturgical routine than that undertaken by the choir-monks, both provided a satisfying spiritual life for the lay-brothers and meant that the work essential to the survival of a large community could be done without hiring outside labour or using peasant rents to pay for it. The emptiness of the countryside where the Cistercians settled and the large tracts of land the monks were given meant that lay-brothers were soon living on farms ('granges' was the Cistercian word) quite far from the abbey, returning for Sunday Mass unless, as was later often the case, the grange was too far away even for this. Walter Espec's original Rievaulx endowment of a few hundred acres became in a short time, because of his generosity and that of other local landowners, many thousands of acres, including most of Bilsdale and much more besides.

The very oldest buildings that survive, badly ruined, at Rievaulx are the remains of the lay-brothers' range, a line of quite modest rooms on the west side of the cloister. Only the broken walls of the ground floor of this range are left; there would, no doubt, have been a long room on the upper floor for the lay-brothers to sleep in. It is not difficult to imagine the tough, cheerful characters who lived and worked here, happy to be part of this thrilling new enterprise – so simple and so holy in its priorities – that had attracted them to leave their families, their fields, their ordinary prospects of wives and child-ren, to dedicate their lives to its service.

The building of the church took many years. The size of the project must have astonished the people of Helmsley and the small, scattered neighbouring settlements, with their modest parish churches. The building stone came from a quarry the monks cut from the limestone daleside, about a quarter of a mile up the Rye from the site chosen for the church.

The monks had little choice as to this site, and it was always tricky for building, in the end needing extensive terracing (with no earth-moving machi-nery). The boundary of Walter Espec's original grant of land was the river itself, and the river then flowed not, as it does now, under Ashberry Hill at the far side of the valley, but down the centre of the flat, glacial valley floor. The monks dug a short canal from the quarry almost to the building-site, so as to float the stone down as far as possible.

These chunks of stone, some of them still there on the outside of the rubble-filled bases of the nave piers, are massive. The quarry and the canal, always damp but full of water only after wet weather, can still be seen if you walk through the stable-yard a little up the road from the abbey car park and follow the footpath signposted to Bow Bridge. To imagine the quarry alive with noise and work, monks and lay-brothers with picks and chisels, mallets and ropes, cutting out and rough-dressing the stone, loading it on to flat wooden rafts to be prodded and coaxed along the canal, is to get very close to the bustle and energy of these first years at Rievaulx.

3

St Aelred

Rievaulx Abbey in summer

One of the young monks hard at work here in the late 1130s was to become the most famous of all English Cistercian abbots, a saint loved and venerated to this day in the Catholic world, and a writer of books that were copied and read all over medieval Christendom. Several of them are in print, in a number of languages, eight and a half centuries later, because they are full of the vivid and deeply attractive life of the spirit that he led in this valley as monk and abbot.

Aelred of Rievaulx left a life of shining promise in the world of courts and kings to join the community at Rievaulx in 1134, when the monastery was only in the third year of its existence and its stone buildings had scarcely been begun. He was a young man of twenty-four, an Anglo-Saxon from old Northumbria, his life already shaped by much of the history outlined in the first chapter.

His grandfather was one of the Durham priests who had fled to Lindisfarne with St Cuthbert's relics to escape the worst of William the Conqueror's harrying of the north. His father, when Benedictine monks took over the daily liturgical duties of the cathedral at Durham in the 1080s, went north to live in Hexham on the Tyne, where what was left of St Wilfrid's great stone church, much knocked about by Vikings, needed care and restoration. Aelred's father spent the rest of his life as curate of the Hexham parish, living in reasonable amity alongside the canons despatched by Archbishop Thurstan to restore regular (semi-monastic) life in Hexham. This was a clash between the old Anglo-Saxon Church of married priests, hereditary responsibilities, and a long tradition of devotion to the saints of the north, and the new, reformed world of celibate clergy, the high moral tone of the twelfth-century Church, and

Norman efficiency. (Thurstan was born in Bayeux and probably educated in Caen, William's Norman capital. He was himself a priest's son, but as Henry I's archbishop of York, from 1114, he had taken the papal reform of the Church fully on board.)

Aelred was brought up in an atmosphere of ancient piety and loyalty to the past. When he was fifteen he was taken into the household of King David of Scotland, at Roxburgh, not far from the North Tyne, to be the companion of the king's son, Prince Henry, and his two older half-brothers. This was a remarkable period of civilized and seriously Christian life at the Scottish court, a pause in the generally bloodthirsty story of the medieval kings of Scotland. King David's father was Shakespeare's Malcolm, who had to mop up Scotland after the horrors of Macbeth's reign; his mother, St Margaret of Scotland, was a cousin of Edward the Confessor. Among many other good works, she had refounded St Columba's monastery on Iona. The atmosphere of warm family friendliness, kindness to the poor, devotion to the sacraments and prayer, and also to books and reading, in which the boy from Hexham found himself, marked him for the rest of his life. Waldef, one of the king's stepsons, ten years older than Aelred, had already become prior of Walter Espec's house of Augustinian canons at Kirkham, not far from Rievaulx, when Aelred was sent by the king, in 1134, on a mission to Archbishop Thurstan in York. Perhaps from Thurstan, perhaps from Waldef, most likely from both, Aelred heard of the new community that had begun monastic life at Rievaulx two years before. On his way back to Scotland, he stayed the night at Helmsley castle with Walter Espec, visited Rievaulx the next morning, could not bear to leave for Scotland, stayed a second night at the castle, returned to Rievaulx the following morning, and, after the four days' wait prescribed by St Benedict for those wanting to become monks, joined the community in which he was to live for the rest of his life.

If Rievaulx, among all the Cistercian abbeys reduced to ruin by Henry VIII, has an atmosphere of gentleness and tranquillity all its own, it is because the spirit of St Aelred has never left it. The stages of his monastic life, the different kinds of work he was given to do by Abbot William and then by his whole monastery, are quickly told. In 1136, as the young community prayed and worked, cleared the valley and hills for farming, and built their abbey, two foundations of new monasteries were made, one at Warden in Bedfordshire (another of Walter Espec's estates) and one, under the auspices of King David, at Melrose in Scotland (where Waldef, now himself a Cistercian, was to become abbot after a time at Rievaulx). There were already enough monks at Rievaulx for twelve of them, and a new abbot, to be sent out for each foundation. Aelred stayed at Rievaulx, sharing the rigours and devotion of the abbey's life with the other novices and junior monks.

In 1143 he was made novice-master, responsible for the earliest formation of new monks joining the community, and at the end of the same year he was sent off as abbot of Rievaulx's third daughter-house, the monastery of Revesby in Lincolnshire. But the most significant event of this part of his life had taken place in 1142, when Abbot William trusted him with a complicated diplomatic mission that sent him all the way to Rome.

A tremendous row had begun in York over the election of a successor to Archbishop Thurstan, who had died in 1140. Waldef, and various other suitable candidates, had been turned down by King Stephen, at the time in chronic conflict with his (and King David's) cousin Queen Matilda over who should rule England. Stephen's candidate seemed quite impossible to most Yorkshire churchmen, and his election looked thoroughly corrupt. Aelred was sent to Rome, with the Archdeacon of York, to put the opposition case to the Pope. The row was to simmer on for more than ten years, and we shall meet its effect on Cistercian life at Fountains in due course. For Aelred what was important was his journey, and above all his meeting, on his way, with Bernard at Clairvaux. They talked at length. The quality of this young English monk struck Bernard forcibly. Bernard told him to write a book, and told him what to call it.

Aelred's *The Mirror of Love* is a beautiful book. Profoundly Christian in both thought and feeling, it uses constant quotation from the Bible – the daily reading of monks always – to support its description of love harnessed to the will of God in the life of an unusually compassionate and acutely intuitive person living in community with many others. There is much of the spirit of St Augustine here – 'my Augustine', as Aelred called him – and of the writer of the *Confessions* rather than the great theologian. A rare understanding of the happiness of a tempered soul, that, not without anguish and suffering, has learnt to cope constructively with deep emotion, and knows that there is always more to learn, is what breathes from Aelred's pages.

He always rated the value of chaste friendship very highly – he was later to write another marvellous book, *On Spiritual Friendship* – but he was also always aware of its dangers, and of the necessity to sustain through prayer the discernment and restraint that would hold friendship safe in God and make of human love an uncluttered path to greater knowledge of the love of God.

It is permissible to guess that Bernard, one of the greatest monastic superiors in the whole history of the Church, told Aelred to write his first book at least partly for the sake of the young monk himself. In any case, *The Mirror of Love*, ever since, has seemed to many the very epitome of early Cistercian monastic life: warm, open to the difficult depths of human experience, and, in an old classical sense (there is a good deal of Cicero in Aelred's writing on friendship), civilized in its balance and moderation. It is also the very first book by an Englishman that gives us a picture of its author's secret heart.

In 1145 Abbot William died, his great achievement at Rievaulx marked by the shrine (now, of course, in pieces) on the left of the chapter-house door. The community elected as their second abbot a learned monk named Maurice who, before coming to Rievaulx, had been the Benedictine sub-prior of Durham. But less than two years later he resigned, since he had been summoned to Fountains as abbot to sort out a crisis in that monastery. The monks of Rievaulx in 1147 chose Aelred as their third abbot. He returned from Revesby and, until his death exactly twenty years later, ruled the monastery with such wisdom and generosity of spirit, in spite of increasing illness and, often, acute pain, that Rievaulx became the most celebrated, as well as the biggest, monastic community in England.

While Aelred was abbot, most of the buildings we now see at Rievaulx were finished, though not the two most impressive ruins: the refectory, built soon after his death, and the lovely Gothic choir, built about fifty years later. But the site of the plain altar, a little east of the crossing, where Aelred said Mass for his monks can easily be imagined, and the chapter-house where every day the monks met for the reading of a chapter of St Benedict's Rule, and for discussion of the community's affairs, is Aelred's own. He was buried here, and only later, when he was acclaimed as a saint, was his coffin moved to behind the high altar of the new choir, where his shrine was looted and smashed by Henry VIII's Dissolution commissioners.

All Cistercian abbots had to travel a good deal. The unity and discipline of the order depended on the connections sustained between mother-houses and their daughter-abbeys. So Aelred, when he was well enough, travelled to Clairvaux, to Warden, Melrose and Revesby, and to Dundrennan and Rufford, two further Rievaulx foundations, every year. He was also in constant demand as an adviser and conciliator in church disputes and problems. He wrote many letters, to kings and popes as well as to abbots and monks, and several more books, including a splendid account of the Battle of the Standard that had taken place in 1138. This would have been a painful subject for him, since this fierce engagement between English and Scottish armies which took place fifteen miles from Rievaulx involved old friends of his on both sides – King David and Prince Henry leading the Scots, while Walter Espec, with Thurstan's support, led the English.

In 1163 Aelred travelled to London for an occasion fraught with sentiment and drama. He preached the sermon in Westminster Abbey for the translation of the relics of St Edward the Confessor, the last Anglo-Saxon king of England and the founder of the Westminster Benedictine community. For Aelred this was an act of piety, coloured by the memories of his boyhood in King David's court. But listening to him were the brilliant young Plantagenet king of England, Henry II, who ruled over more of France than the French king, and his new Archbishop of Canterbury, Thomas Becket. They were still on speaking terms, but only just. The murder that scandalized Christendom was seven years in the future.

None of this work ever deflected Aelred from his first task, which was to rule his monks with fairness, perception and love, for the good of each one, and for the good of the whole community. He was a wonderful example of a lived-out Cistercian vocation at its very best, and every visitor to Rievaulx should remember him with some of the affection he inspired in all those who knew him when he was alive.

Walter Daniel, the monk who wrote *The Life of Aelred*, who knew him well and was present at his death, wrote:

> He turned the house of Rievaulx into a stronghold for the sustaining of the weak, the nourishment of the strong and whole. [Here he is consciously echoing the Rule of St Benedict.] It was the home of piety and peace, the abode of perfect love of God and neighbour. Who was there, however despised and rejected, who did not find a loving father in Aelred and timely comforters in the brethren? . . . 'All,' Aelred would say, 'whether weak or strong, should find in Rievaulx a place of peace, and there, like the fish in the broad seas, possess the welcome, happy, spacious peace of love.'

After Aelred's death the Rievaulx community prospered for another century or so. The wool from the Rievaulx sheep-runs, where lay-brother shepherds lived through icy winters in the moorland granges and sheared the flocks in summer, was the best in Europe, keenly sought after by the pernickety weavers of Italy and Flanders. Iron ore was worked in Bilsdale. Nearer home, the abbey grew its own corn and vegetables (Yorkshire Cistercians invented the greenhouse), painted and fired its own tiles, milled its corn (the old mill in the village, now a house, has medieval stonework in its walls), brewed its beer, fished its ponds (three remain above the mill, and one by the cricket pitch), grazed its cattle and tanned their hides (brick tanning-troughs survive in the lowest range of abbey buildings).

If you walk back from Bow Bridge along the valley floor towards the abbey, you will get a faint, fractured impression of how it would have struck a traveller in the thirteenth century: at a turn in the folds of the northern hills, suddenly he would see a great assemblage of stone buildings, stepped on the slope of the dale above the river, a cross between a large farm and an Oxford college, with a church the size of a cathedral at its back. And inside the complex of buildings was always the quiet cloister, monks copying books in the scriptorium or walking in silent prayer, all gathered in the choir for Mass and to sing the Office every day and every night.

A number of blows then fell on the community:

epidemics of terrible sheep disease; mounting debt; the plundering of the abbey by a Scottish army in 1322; in the 1340s the national tragedy of the Black Death, at its most virulent in monasteries; a gradual decline in Cistercian fervour and vocations; a more rapid decline in the number of lay-brothers. Tenants now did the work lay-brothers had once done. The chapter-house was made smaller. The old infirmary became a grand house for the abbot to entertain his guests in. There were no serious scandals. But when the king's men arrived in 1538, to bring to a sudden end the monastic life faithfully lived at Rievaulx for four centuries, they met with no resistance. Twenty-two monks took their modest pensions and disappeared into secular life, and only the ruins were left to remind us of the men whose blessed home this was, and, above all, of the great abbot who prayed and worked and wrote in this place.

4

Fountains Abbey

Fountains Abbey from the west

Fountains Abbey is one of the most beautiful, one of the most visited, and probably the most carefully studied of all the ruined monasteries of Europe. No one who has been there is likely to forget the experience of walking across the wide green lawn from the west towards these extraordinary buildings: the bare west front of the abbey church, with its tall fourteenth-century window; the stark twelfth-century nave with the noble sixteenth-century tower behind and to the north of it; and the long, low lay-brothers' range with its plain round-arched windows and great, dark doorways. Inside the lay-brothers' range, now a single stone-vaulted space nearly 300 feet long, the impression is even more astonishing. And the soaring east end of the church, the chapel of the nine altars, built on the scale of a major cathedral in the thirteenth century, still awaits the visitor. This was the richest and most splendidly built of all English Cistercian abbeys, but its beginning was full of pain, anguish and bitter resolve.

The warm, confident openness of Aelred's Rievaulx, so well described by Walter Daniel, should not blur in our imagination the bracing rigour of its, and all, early Cistercian life. The complete fidelity to St Benedict's Rule, the extra austerity of a regime which had every monk rising, in his habit, from his sleeping-mat in a huge cold dormitory for Matins at 1.30 a.m. every night of the year; which allowed no meat to be eaten, and no bath to be taken, ever, except in the infirmary by the old and ill; which buried its dead without coffins or marked graves; which had every monk taking a daily part in the manual labour of the community; which regarded as essential the monastic silence; which excluded lay people altogether from church and cloister – all this was felt as a challenge, a reproach, and on occasion a threat, by the established Benedictine monasteries of the time. The Cistercian example sometimes inspired the most fervent members of an older community to press for reforms at home; it could then become a danger to both obedience and unity. We have already met Maurice, a distinguished Benedictine who left the cathedral priory at Durham for Rievaulx, later to become its second abbot. Durham cannot have been happy to see him go. A grave crisis in another Benedictine community delivered, after some dreadful scenes of monastic dissension, the second Yorkshire Cistercian abbey.

In June 1132, less than four months after the arrival of Abbot William and his companions in the valley of the Rye, thirteen Benedictine monks of St Mary's Abbey, York, led by Richard, the prior of the monastery, and a second Richard, the sacrist, went to their abbot and asked for wide-ranging reform in the life of their community. They realised that not every aspect of Cistercian life was practicable in a city-centre abbey, but they wanted, at least, to restore proper Benedictine observance of silence, a plain, meatless diet, and enclosure (choir-monks living in the monastery and not behaving like country gentlemen on far-flung estates). The abbot, an old man and not a strong character, panicked. He failed to respond to the call for reform, failed to pull his community together, sent for Archbishop Thurstan to arbitrate, objected to the strong team of clerics Thurstan brought to St Mary's, and eventually had to let his reformers go – only, in the first place, as far as Thurstan's house, where the archbishop gave them refuge. A characteristically firm intervention from Clairvaux by Bernard, to whom the poor abbot had appealed for help, confirmed the renegades in their resolve and thanked Thurstan for his help.

After two months with Thurstan, and the loss back to St Mary's of two of their number but the gain of two more Benedictines, this time from Whitby, Prior Richard's little group were taken by the archbishop to Ripon, his own church, for a Christmas Mass, and then given the wild valley of Skeldale to make the best of as their new monastic home. Their first winter was very hard: they had nothing to eat but the food charitably sent them by Thurstan; they had to make their own chapel and huts for shelter and plant their first vegetable garden; they had no lay-brothers to help them. This was Cistercian austerity with a vengeance. They persevered. They soon asked Bernard for formal admission to the Cistercian order. He not only granted this willingly, to the two monks who had travelled to Clairvaux with the request, but sent back with them a wise old monk of long experience to help the little community become in all respects accustomed to Cistercian life. By the winter of 1134–5, however, they were still so poor that their abbot, the first Richard, who had been prior at St Mary's, went to Clairvaux to beg a French site where things might be a little easier. In his absence the tide for what was now Fountains Abbey, though still without stone buildings or any secure future, turned for good.

Hugh, the Dean of York, one of Thurstan's band of powerful clerics in the original confrontation at St Mary's, arrived at Fountains as a novice. Perhaps he had not been able to shed the impression made on him by the evident holiness of the men who had so much wanted to make a new and better monastic start. In any case, his arrival made all the difference. He was a rich and scholarly man. He brought with him considerable wealth, land to add to the monastery's endowment, and his library. He was soon followed by two more rich canons of York Minster, equally inspired to reform their own spiritual lives. These three departures from his cathedral chapter must have had Thurstan's blessing. At last there was confidence at Fountains. Real building began. Recruits appeared, both choir-monks and lay-brothers. By 1139 the community was big enough to have founded three daughter-houses. The abbots of these new foundations were all monks of the original Benedictine group. One of them, Robert of Newminster, in Northumberland, was a visionary from Whitby Abbey who, after his death in 1159 was acclaimed as a saint, the only Fountains monk ever to be so venerated.

But the troubles of Fountains were by no means over. Abbot Richard I died in Rome in 1139, and was succeeded by the second Richard, the sacrist from St Mary's. A mild contemplative, whose holiness was never forgotten in his abbey, he was an anxious and muddled administrator who found the task of building a whole monastery too much for him. Four times he asked to retire and was refused. In 1143 death released him from responsibilities he could not cope with. His successor proved to be a mixed blessing. A protégé of Bernard, Henry Murdac was a Yorkshire-man who had trained in the monastic life at Clairvaux itself. He was a tough organizer and had already ruled over a new Cistercian abbey in France.

Murdac arrived at Fountains in 1144 to find a small stone church and the monks still living in wooden buildings. In three years of energetic work he built stone ranges for monks and lay-brothers to the east and west of a large new cloister, and he began to enlarge the church. These are the oldest buildings you can see at Fountains today, though all are difficult to discern from the later building that encases them. But Abbot Henry was already em-broiled in the fiercely contended issue of who should be Thurstan's successor as Archbishop of York. Bernard, now pulling many a string in Christendom, and Pope Eugenius III (one of Bernard's monk-pupils) wanted to replace King Stephen's archbishop with Abbot Henry. So angry did this make the York supporters of the king's archbishop that in 1146 they came to Fountains to kill the abbot. When they failed to find him (he was flat on his face, praying in the sanctuary), they looted the abbey, though there was not much to steal, and set fire to the brand-new buildings. The following year Henry Murdac never-theless became Archbishop of York.

The community at Fountains may have been thankful to see the back of Abbot Henry, his energy and efficiency notwithstanding. But the calm rule of an abbot who was both a good monk and a capable administrator did not come their way until Richard, abbot of Vauclair in France, arrived in 1150. Managing Fountains after Murdac (and dealing with his interference, from York, in the abbey's affairs) had by then proved too much for two Rievaulx monks, our old friend Maurice, Rievaulx's second abbot, and Thorold, both of whom resigned the Fountains abbacy in despair.

Under Abbot Richard III a long period of constructive stability began at Fountains. All the buildings we now see standing, except for the tower, were completed in the next hundred years. By the middle of the thirteenth century the reputation of the abbey shone throughout England and further afield. Benefactions of land and the wealth which it brought had poured in. An un-Cistercian spirit of competition with Rievaulx put both abbeys in debt when they built the glorious east ends of their churches. From the fourteenth century onwards the monastery at Fountains suffered the same slow attrition as Rievaulx, its first model and inspiration: sheep disease, plundering Scottish soldiers, the gradual disappearance of lay-brothers, and a more comfortable life for fewer and fewer choir-monks. Abbot Huby, early in the sixteenth century, built the tower – a gesture of architectural splendour that would have appalled

Bernard of Clairvaux. Huby died in 1526, when Cardinal Wolsey was in charge of England and Henry VIII was still married to Catherine of Aragon. At the Dissolution, thirteen years later, thirty-one monks and the last abbot (Marmaduke Bradley, a featherer of his own nest who had schemed to get rid of his predecessor and managed to emerge from Henry VIII's reign in lucrative charge of Ripon Minster) meekly resigned Fountains to the king.

Fountains Abbey was one of the great medieval enterprises of northern England, by far the richest Cistercian monastery in the whole country, a civilizing influence deep into the moors and fells of the Yorkshire Dales, and for four centuries home to generations of monks.

There was never an Aelred at Fountains. But one twelfth-century abbot deserves to be particularly remembered for the quality both of his spiritual life and of his serene leadership of his community. Ralph Haget resisted his vocation to the monastic life until he was nearly thirty. Then he became a monk at Fountains, and was elected abbot of Kirkstall and then abbot of Fountains. He was the eighth abbot of Fountains, but the first both to make his profession and to die in the monastery. He once told his monks that, in prayer, he had seen and understood the fear of God, but had not been afraid. This is a piercing summary of monastic courage and peace. At his death in 1203 the heroic Cistercian century was over.

5

Byland Abbey

Byland: the west door of the abbey church

When the first Cistercians left Molesme Abbey in 1098 for the Burgundian hills, other monks eager for a strict and frugal life had collected, in a more scattered and random fashion, in the woods of Maine, over to the west in the dukedom of Normandy. One gathering of these monks became the monastery of Savigny, founded in 1112 (the year that Bernard arrived at Cîteaux) by a Norman hermit called Vitalis. The life lived at Savigny was very like that of the early Cistercians, but, without the clarity of the *Carta Caritatis*, foundations and connections between mother and daughter houses were more haphazard and trouble-prone.

A Savignac abbey was established at Furness in Cumbria by 1127. In 1134 a group of its monks made a new foundation at Calder, further north on the exposed north-west coast. In 1137, the year before the Battle of the Standard, King David of Scotland allowed his terrifying Galloway Picts to run wild at the new abbey, and the monks fled back to Furness, where they were not welcome. Two abbots under the same roof is never easy. The Calder monks decided to cross the Pennines and appeal to Archbishop Thurstan for help.

As we know, they were not the first monastic splinter-group to be supported at a moment of crisis by this remarkable man. On this occasion the refugee monks, with one ox-cart containing all their books and habits, and no other possessions, were given a place to live at Hood, near Thirsk, by a noble and holy lady, Gundreda, the widowed mother of Roger de Mowbray, an important Norman lord. Gundreda was a friend and penitent of Thurstan's.

When more monks and lay-brothers joined the rescued community and they needed a better site than

Hood, Thurstan and Gundreda persuaded Roger de Mowbray to give them a stretch of the Rye valley above Rievaulx. Here they moved in 1143, but they were much too close to Rievaulx for comfort – the monks could hear each other's bells, and the lay-brothers were no doubt soon squabbling about whose cattle were muddying the river and upsetting the fish. (Not long after this the Rievaulx monks moved the Rye – always the boundary between Espec and Mowbray land – to its present course close under Ashberry wood, to give Rievaulx the benefit of all the flat fields at the valley bottom.) In 1147 Roger de Mowbray transferred the Savignacs from Old Byland to a site at Stocking, near Coxwold. From here, thirty years later, the community moved to its final home, Byland Abbey.

In the momentous year of 1147 Aelred became abbot of Rievaulx, Henry Murdac left Fountains to become Archbishop of York, and at the Cîteaux General Chapter Bernard and the abbot of Cîteaux granted the request of the abbot of Savigny for all his somewhat confused monasteries, unsure of which abbot was responsible for what, to be absorbed into the clear structure of the Cistercian order. So as the Byland monks moved to a reasonable distance from Rievaulx (though they were still a good deal closer than the fifteen miles specified by Cistercian regulations) they became part of the same great, and now extraordinarily successful and well organized, family of monks.

The abbey at Byland has a different atmosphere from the much more considerable ruins at Rievaulx and Fountains. There is more room, more air; the lay-out of the monastery is easier for the visitor to grasp, and there seems to be a more spacious tidiness in its design. There are three reasons for this. The first is that the site was chosen and cleared and the abbey was planned and largely built (only the church remained to be finished) before the community moved in from Stocking, a couple of miles away.

The second reason is that here it was possible, late in the Cistercian century, with the benefit of other abbeys' experience, for the monks to plan their monastery for a large community (80 monks and 140 lay-brothers) on a site big enough for each building to be the right size and in the proper Cistercian relation to others. Both Rievaulx and Fountains are in narrow valleys. Both abbeys solved problems with levels and the course of their rivers in ways that add much to their architectural interest, but both had to alter and adapt their buildings several times over the years.

The third reason for the sense of lucid order that the ruins of Byland still have may well be the influence on the whole building operation of this community's own great twelfth-century abbot. Roger of Byland, a young monk in the harassed years at Calder, was elected abbot when the impoverished wanderers were still at Hood in 1142. He retired from the job, a very old man, in 1196. He saw the young community through four moves and then into its golden period at the end of the century, when Rievaulx, Fountains and Byland were said by a contemporary writer (William of Malmesbury) to be, equally, the shining lights of monastic life in the north. Roger was revered for the rest of Byland's history as its real founding abbot. He was a wise, kindly and resolute man who kept his monks together through trying times, who established, with some difficulty and with Aelred's help, the independence of his house from Furness and strengthened its connection with Savigny, and who accepted the haven of the Cistercian order for his monks with warmth and enthusiasm. He became a devoted friend of Aelred, and anointed him on his deathbed.

Byland Abbey never achieved the fame of Rievaulx or the wealth of Fountains. Its later history was a quieter version of theirs. After its complicated start, which must have severely tested the vocations of its early monks, it settled down to a peaceful, uneventful life, suffering the troubles of each century that afflicted all these northern houses, but surviving them all in good, though modest, order. It is an excellent place to absorb something of the undemonstrative dedication of most monks' lives and deaths, remembered only in their own communities and in the eternity of God. The Byland church, in particular – the largest Cistercian church in England when it was built, and architecturally the most adventurous – is still beautiful and very moving, with its broken rose window at the west end and the fine geometrical patterns of its tiles in the south transept (the walls of this transept collapsed only in 1822).

At the Dissolution in 1538 the abbot and twenty-five monks surrendered the house without open complaint. In the little museum at the abbey the broken base of the chapter-house lectern, from which the Rule was read daily for centuries, suggests not only the stability and obedience in which sons and daughters of St Benedict have always undertaken to live, but also the sadness of the end when it came. The pen and inkwell are probably those used by the last abbot to sign away his monastery to the king.

6

Jervaulx Abbey

Jervaulx chapter-house

Fifteen miles above Ripon in the middle of
Wensleydale, where the wide River Ure flows gently
through fertile meadows, Jervaulx Abbey, more
ruined and on a smaller scale than the other three
Cistercian monasteries of the old North Riding, is not
far from Fountains. But Jervaulx's early connections
were with Byland.

In 1145 half a dozen men, led by a gifted doctor

called Peter de Quincy, had been given by the grateful Earl of Richmond (whose life de Quincy had saved) a little rough land at Fors, further up the Ure near Aysgarth, to try monastic life under the distant auspices of Savigny. In the following year they received instructions from Savigny that they were to regard themselves as under the authority of the abbot of Byland, the nearest Savignac community, at the time still at Old Byland, close to Rievaulx. Although he had plenty of problems to deal with at home, Abbot Roger of Byland did not neglect his new charge. He helped the group at Fors into the Cistercian order along with Byland in 1147. Three years later, realising that they were losing heart in their harsh moorland home, he sent them nine Byland monks to stiffen the community and set them on a more confident monastic path. In 1156 the fortunes of the house took a decisive turn for the better. The young Earl of Richmond, honouring his father's commitment to this still tentative religious project, gave the monks a splendid new site at Jervaulx, and he and others generously endowed the abbey with productive land. By the early thirteenth century, Jervaulx owned half of Wensleydale, from the abbey up to the source of the river, including the whole parish of Aysgarth, the largest in England. Corn, cattle (cheese, naturally), horses and, of course, sheep were grown and tended and produced profitably by lay-brothers and later by tenants. The abbey was England's third largest wool-producer by the late thirteenth century (after Fountains and Rievaulx), and its income at the Dissolution was close to Byland's.

This wealth and security supported for nearly 400 years a community moderate in size and orderly in its way of life. Its buildings, put up according to the usual Cistercian plan in the second half of the twelfth century and little altered thereafter, were like Byland's exactly contemporary buildings in design, though in all respects on a reduced scale. The church, ruined almost to ground level, must have been very fine. Two poignant reminders of the silenced routine of the Mass and Office sung here by the monks through all those years are the stone altar in the north transept, with its five incised crosses for the wounds of Christ still clear and crisp, and the damaged effigy of Henry FitzHugh, a pious benefactor of the abbey buried here in 1307 so that his bones should lie where the monks would always pray.

The long west range, where the lay-brothers lived and worked, is a smaller and much more ruined version of the same kind of building at Fountains. Now it has only a few bare arched windows left, and the bases of the columns to suggest the stone vaulting that once carried the upper floor. The most substantial buildings that remain at Jervaulx are the high lancet-windowed wall of the monks' dormitory, in its usual position to the south-east of the cloister, and, a little further to the south-east, a wall of the monks' infirmary, built a little later and with grander windows to its raised hall. But the building which most clearly suggests the daily life of the monks is the chapter-house, as always on the east side of the cloister. Its two splendid Romanesque windows on to the cloister, one each side of the door and its steps, survive, as do five of its octagonal columns, each made of a single length of stone, with carved capitals. This was the room which saw the noblest moment in Jervaulx's history.

In 1535 Henry VIII had declared himself to be Supreme Head of the Church in England in order to take the Church out of its ancient obedience to the Pope. An act of Parliament had been passed declaring the royal supremacy, and all the clergy in England were being asked for their assent. Mostly, led by almost all the bishops, they gave it. A preacher of the royal supremacy, accompanied by a tearaway young Yorkshire squire called Sir Francis Bigod, arrived at Jervaulx on 12 July, six days after the execution of Sir Thomas More in London for refusing assent to the royal supremacy. While the preacher was putting the king's case in the chapter-house, a monk interrupted. He declared that he 'neither could nor would take the King's highness for to be the only and supreme head of the Church of England' and that he 'thanked God who gave him spirit and audacity to say so'. After the rest of the community had signed the king's paper, Bigod bundled this monk off to Middleham Castle and bullied him, in vain, to change his mind. He was tried at York assizes on

6 August and was soon afterwards executed. His name was George Lazenby and he was the only martyr for the Catholic faith among all the Yorkshire Cistercians.

In the following year the Pilgrimage of Grace, the northern rising against the dissolution of the lesser monasteries by the king, pulled the unwilling abbot of Jervaulx, Adam Sedbergh, into its choppy wake. A mob of peasants arrived at the abbey demanding the abbey's support for the rebellion. The abbot fled into the fells and only reappeared four days later when the monks seemed about to be forced to depose him. A few months later both he and the ex-abbot of Fountains (manoeuvred out of his job by crafty Marmaduke Bradley, and living quietly at Jervaulx) were victims of a rapid piece of blackmail inflicted on them by two more threatening rebels. Both these old abbots were swept up in the king's savage revenge for the Pilgrimage of Grace. Neither was guilty of anything more serious than indecision and incompetence. Both were found guilty of treason and were hanged, drawn and quartered in London in the summer of 1537. (Francis Bigod, who had raised a side-show rebellion of his own but not to save the abbeys, was executed on the same day as the abbot of Jervaulx.)

Because of the 'treason' of their abbot, the Jervaulx monks were swiftly dispossessed of their monastery and sent off into the world with no pensions. The abbey was not only stripped of its lead and looted in the usual Dissolution fashion, but was also dynamited. Hence the almost complete destruction of the church. Abbot Sedbergh's exquisite wooden screen and stall from the church, carved in Ripon in about 1520, were rescued by someone, and can be seen to this day in the Aysgarth parish church.

One Jervaulx monk, whose name was Thomas Madde and who lived until 1579, when Queen Elizabeth had been on the throne for more than twenty years, is recorded as saying that he 'did take away and hide the head of one of his brethren of the same house, who had suffered death for that he would not yield to the Royal Supremacy.' So the memory of George Lazenby lived on into the time when Shakespeare would write of the 'Bare ruin'd choirs where late the sweet birds sang.'

By then, of course, there was not one monastery left in the whole of England. The last English monks had gone to France and Flanders, a few of them risking their lives to minister to Catholic recusants. But their communities were not to return to England until driven home by the French Revolution.

7

Postscript

Fountains Abbey from the east

After the Dissolution the Cistercian abbeys were, for at least two centuries, no more than stone-quarries for local people. (An altar-stone from Byland, recognized by its five crosses, was found in a local farmyard in the nineteenth century. It is now an altar in the abbey church at Ampleforth.) The commissioners left the abbeys open to the weather. The lead from their roofs was taken to sell for the king. Usually it was melted into bars in pits fired by the burning of the rafters. Henry VIII had, for a passing moment, considered saving the church at Fountains to be a new cathedral. He chose Chester instead. The ruins crumbled slowly and became ivy-covered, the homes of owls and pigeons. Confident, Protestant England, assembling its empire, leaving the despised 'Middle Ages' behind, was not interested in abbeys.

In the neo-classical early eighteenth century, when rich Englishmen with a taste for the Virgilian 'sublime' looked about their estates for ruins that might make of every prospect a Poussin or a Claude picture, one or two were lucky enough to find they already had a magnificent specimen in their possession.

In the 1720s and 1730s John Aislabie, wealthy but in disgrace after the South Sea Bubble burst, laid out in Skeldale a formal garden, moving mountains of earth and organizing the river into lakes and canals, with the ruins of Fountains at the end of his vista. Classical temples dotted his landscape; he did no actual damage to the abbey. But his son William, in the new informal taste of the second half of the century, bought Fountains for a huge sum of money in order to incorporate the ruins in his garden and adjust them to his idea of picturesque Gothic. He did some good but more harm to the abbey. His contemporary at Helmsley, Thomas Duncombe, fortunately did no more to Rievaulx than to construct a fine grassy terrace, with his own classical temples, above the abbey, from which his guests could appreciate his ruin from different points of view.

The Victorians treated medieval ruins in the spirit of serious historical enquiry rather than landscape design. The park laid out at Jervaulx in the mid-nineteenth century gently frames the abbey without 'using' it insensitively, and at this period all the landowners responsible for these abbeys began to allow and even encourage the beginnings of careful excavation and preservation. At the end of the twentieth century English Heritage cares for Rievaulx, Fountains and Byland with expert concern for their conservation and admirable clarity in their explanation for visitors. If Jervaulx, still managed privately, has a special appeal in its lack of labels, its rambler roses and honeysuckle, we must remember that this is a romantic presentation of a medieval abbey, really no closer to actual Cistercian life than the neat gravel paths and helpful plans of the public authority.

To learn about this life we must depend upon two things. One is the words and the stories of monks and those who helped them to live, their whole lives devoted to God, in these wonderful places. The other is the long continuity, the continuing presence in our world, of monastic life itself.

The heroes of our account of the Yorkshire

Cistercians are not only the great abbots and monks – Aelred of Rievaulx and Richard of Fountains, Roger of Byland and George Lazenby of Jervaulx – but also Archbishop Thurstan, without whom none of these communities might have got properly started, St Bernard of Clairvaux, the inspiration and strength of the Cistercian twelfth century, and behind them all St Benedict, whose Rule provided and provides the framework for the daily life of all western monks.

The words of St Aelred, preaching to his monks on St Benedict in the 1150s, ring as true now for the monks of Ampleforth Abbey (six miles from Rievaulx and three miles from Byland) as they have rung, for eight and a half centuries, for all monks, and for anyone else attempting a serious Christian life:

> At the beginning of his new way of life, our holy father St Benedict found the road narrow, but at the end he found it very wide. What did he do when he found it narrow? Did he turn aside from it? By no means; rather, he held to it and persevered in it boldly. In his Rule he urges that no one should fly from the way of salvation because of fear. It is a road which can only be entered upon as a narrow path, as experience had taught him. For he knew that although it was very narrow, it would lead to life. It is by this road that St Benedict passed from death to life, from Egypt to the Promised Land, that is from the darkness of this world to Jerusalem, which is the vision of peace.

Let us too, dear brothers, pass over to this wonderful sight. Let us follow in the steps of our holy father Benedict. We have the straightest of roads by which to arrive there: his Rule and his teaching. If we keep to it as we ought and persevere in it, without any doubt we, too, shall come to the place where he is.

Further Reading

David Knowles, *The Monastic Order in England*, Cambridge University Press, 1963.

David Knowles, *The Religious Orders in England Vol. III*, Cambridge University Press, 1971.

Stephen Tobin, *The Cistercians*, Herbert Press, 1995.

Aelred Squire, *Aelred of Rievaulx*, SPCK, 1969.

Walter Daniel, *The Life of Ailred of Rievaulx*, trans. F. M. Powicke, Nelson, 1950.

Aelred of Rievaulx, *Mirror of Charity*, Cistercian Publications, 1990.

Aelred of Rievaulx, *Spiritual Friendship*, Cistercian Publications, 1977.

Donald Nicholl, *Thurstan, Archbishop of York*, Stonegate Press, 1964.

Glyn Coppack, *Fountains Abbey*, English Heritage/Batsford, 1993.

Excellent short guidebooks, with detailed plans, are available at each abbey.